CW01499973

BAYER 04 LEVERKUSEN: AN INTRODUCTION

2022/23 SEASON

JOHN ALDER

Bayer 04 Leverkusen

An introduction

John Alder

Second edition

© 2021 John Alder

John Alder has asserted his rights in accordance with the Copyright, Designs and Patents Act 1988 to be identified as the author of this work.

Published by Alder Education Limited

First published in eBook format in January 2016

All rights reserved under International and Pan-American Copyright Conventions. By payment of the required fees, you have been granted the non-exclusive, non-transferable right to access and read the text of this e-book on-screen. No part of this text may be reproduced, transmitted, downloaded, decompiled, reverse-engineered, or stored in or introduced into any information storage and retrieval system, in any form or by any means, whether electronic or mechanical, now known or hereinafter invented, without the express written permission of the Publisher.

Table of Contents

❦ Created with Vellum

1

WHY A BOOK ABOUT BAYER 04 LEVERKUSEN?

A historic and successful football club

Bayer 04 Leverkusen was founded in 1904, making it one of Germany's oldest football clubs. A member of the Bundesliga every year since 1979, Leverkusen has ended twenty two of those years in one of the top five places. The club has appeared in the Champions League twelve times and the Europa League seven times.

The perfect introduction to German football

A visit to Bayer 04 Leverkusen is also the perfect starting point for people new to Germany and its football culture:

It is close to two major airports, next to a motorway and easy to reach by public transport.

It has a spectacular, modern stadium which brings every spectator close to the action and to maximise the atmosphere.

The club has one of the most family-friendly set-ups in the Bundesliga.

The team plays an exciting and highly entertaining brand of football.

I want to tell the English-speaking world about the history and tradition of this fantastic club, to describe its triumphs and disappointments, and to tell the life-stories of its more famous players and managers. Of course, I also want to persuade you to come and experience the excitement of German football for yourself.

2

WHAT'S BEHIND THE NAME?

Compared to many German clubs, Bayer 04 Leverkusen has quite a straightforward name.

Bayer refers to the pharmaceutical multinational based in Leverkusen. The club was formed by employees of the company and it has provided substantial financial support over the years. So it is only reasonable for Bayer to get a mention in the name.

The Bayer workers formed the club in 1904, which explains the 04 - and Leverkusen is an industrial town on the Rhine, between Düsseldorf and Cologne.

Of course, it's not as simple as that. In 1904 the Bayer concern was a paint manufacturer, the original club did not play football and the town of Leverkusen did not exist - but all will become clear in the next chapter.

3

A BRIEF HISTORY

The early years

The story of Bayer Leverkusen begins in 1903 with Wilhelm Hauschild and 170 other employees of Bayer, a local paint manufacturer. They wrote a letter to their employer requesting support in setting up a sports club. The company agreed and on 1 July 1904, Turn- und Spielverein Bayer 04 Leverkusen was established.

This club was to be one of the first works sports clubs in Germany. Its first director was Major a.D. Albert Mandel, who was also responsible for staff welfare at the factory.

The large industrial town that we now know as Leverkusen appeared in 1930, following the merger of four distinct communities. In 1904, Leverkusen was a tiny settlement near the Rhine, named after a German industrialist called Carl Leverkus. It found its way into the club name because almost everyone who lived there worked at the Bayer factory.

Bayer would eventually become the multinational pharmaceutical giant we know today, and which still has its headquarters in Leverkusen.

Football only comes later

Turn- und Spielverein means 'gymnastics and games club' and, as the name implies, activities covered a range of sports and games - but not football. Until World War I, gymnastics dominated German sport. Traditionalists were very sceptical about football, which they considered to be an import. Football was, however, rapidly becoming very popular amongst young workers. So in May 1907, 16 young men got together and resolved to request the formation of a football section. After long consideration, the management committee agreed to this, so long as its members also trained with medicine balls at least once a week.

The new team called itself Fußballverein 04 Leverkusen. It had about 150 members, all of whom worked for Bayer. As today, the colours were black and red, and they obtained permission to wear the company logo on their shirts. They played the first fixture in August 1907 against Ballspielverein Manfort.

The club joined the Cologne district league and within four years had gained promotion to the second division.

Nowhere to play

Finding somewhere to play was a major headache for several early German football teams. Because many people did not consider football to be respectable, regular access to a good pitch was very difficult to achieve. This slowed

Leverkusen's progress considerably in the early years as they moved between several temporary venues. It was not until 1910 that the club found a permanent home.

Bayer Leverkusen continued to grow and in May 1914 announced plans to build a new ground. Of course, the outbreak of World War 1 later the same year delayed the implementation of these plans.

Immediately after the war, things were quickly brought back on track, and the team eventually found a home in Leverkusen-Wiesdorf.

Sportvereinigung Bayer 04 Leverkusen

Unlike in Britain, sport in Germany had developed in the late 19th and early 20th centuries through gymnastics. Many traditionalists looked down on team games. Indeed, in the eyes of many, football was not a proper sport at all. In clubs all over Germany, there were heated disagreements between the gymnasts and the footballers. This animosity contributed to an eventual split in the club. But the main reason for the divorce appears to have been the insistence by the German Gymnastics Association that gymnastics and other sports should be separate. So in 1923, the footballers and boxers left to form their own separate club. They were joined in 1927 by the handball and fistball players and the athletes.

The new club called itself Sportvereinigung Bayer 04 Leverkusen. The gymnasts formed their own club called TuS Bayer 04 Leverkusen. Sportvereinigung Bayer 04 Leverkusen kept the traditional colours of red and black.

By 1931, the club had gained promotion to the first division of the Cologne district league and moved to a new ground called "Am Stadtpark", which was to be its home until 1958.

The 1930s and 1940s

The Nazis seize power

In January 1933, the National Socialist Party gained power in Germany and one month later used the burning of the Reichstag as an excuse to suspend the constitution. So began their reign of terror, which was to permeate every single aspect of German life, cause the most destructive war the world has ever seen and ultimately lead to the defeat and destruction of Germany.

Between 1933 and 1945, to have an opinion, or to act on it, or indeed to attract the attention of the authorities in any way, often resulted in arrest, imprisonment, torture and death. A host of fanatical party members, opportunists and informers who enabled the Nazis to impose their system of terror, violence, repression and humiliation.

The tentacles of Nazism reached into every aspect of life. Football, which was no exception, was re-organised into 16 regional leagues called Gauligen. They placed Leverkusen in the Gauliga Niederrhein, along with Borussia Mönchengladbach, Düsseldorf, Essen, Duisburg and Wuppertal. As in all clubs across the country, Jewish players and board members were removed and a new system of management was introduced.

Promotion
In 1936, the club achieved promotion to the second division.

The players wore the Bayer cross on their shirts for the first time at the promotion game against Solingen 95. Almost all the players worked for the company and so wearing the company logo enabled them to show their commitment and loyalty to their employer.

Football continues in the war

Football continued in Germany almost to the end of World War 2. The Nazi government believed that 'business as usual' demonstrated the country's strength and confidence. Crowds continued to grow in Leverkusen and the ground was extended in 1941. As the war came to a close, football had to be abandoned. But once the fighting stopped, Bayer soon started playing competitive fixtures again, dominating local and state leagues.

'Professionalism' arrives

By 1949 Bayer were challenging for promotion to the top flight - the Oberliga West. Unfortunately, in the first of a long series of disappointments and near misses, they lost both play-off games to local rivals 1. FC Köln. Despite this setback, the club went professional. This is not as clear-cut as it seems. For decades, there had been a heated debate about professionalism. Its supporters argued that this was the only way to bring German football up to international standards. Its opponents argued that paying players would diminish sporting ideals and lead to crass commercialism. In the end, the football authorities (the DFB) agreed to a classic compromise. Clubs could pay their players, but only if they had a 'real' job as well. This was perfect for a works team like Bayer Leverkusen where players could have notional employment with the parent company.

The 1950s - promotion and a new stadium

In 1951, Bayer 04 finally achieved promotion to the Oberliga West.

Despite relegation to the second tier five years later, the club began work on a new stadium, which was completed in 1958.

The 1960s and 1970s - near misses and finally promotion

Promotion in 1962 meant a brief return to the Oberliga West, but when the Bundesliga was formed in 1963, Bayer had not accumulated enough points to secure a place in the top division. They came close to promotion in 1968 when they won the regional league. Unfortunately, they lost the play-off round to Offenbacher Kickers.

In 1973, the club was relegated to the amateur district league. Despite emerging as champions the following season, changes to the league structure meant that Leverkusen were not admitted into the 2 Bundesliga. They achieved promotion the following year.

In 1975, the club appointed a new coach - Willibert Kremer. Under his leadership, Leverkusen established itself as a strong professional club. Kremer combined talented youth players with experienced older hands to create a strong squad.

Finally, in 1979, the year of the club's 75th anniversary, promotion to the Bundesliga was achieved. This was undoubtedly the most successful year yet for Leverkusen.

Promotion was secured with five games in hand. Three days later they came back from a 3:0 half time deficit to achieve a draw with rival works team Uerdingen - enough to win the league. By accumulating 59 points that season, Leverkusen set a new league record. They scored the most (87) and conceded the fewest (34) goals.

It is not surprising that fans consumed 3,000 litres of free beer in the anniversary celebrations put on by the club.

The following season, the first Bundesliga game was against Bayern München and although Leverkusen lost 3:1, Dieter Demuth scored the club's first ever Bundesliga goal.

The 1980s and 1990s - the first two trophies and a bigger stadium

Leverkusen continued to develop through the 1980s and in 1988 achieved its greatest success to date, beating Español Barcelona to win the UEFA Cup.

Then, in 1993, Bayer won their first national title, beating Hertha Berlin to win the DFB Cup.

They were also were runners-up in the Bundesliga in 1997.

The Haberland Stadium was expanded and renamed the BayArena.

The next decade cemented Bayer 04's reputation as a club that consistently did well, but just missed out on titles.

1999/2000

Bayer Leverkusen had achieved second place in four of the previous five seasons and their performance in the

1999/2000 season was nothing less than brilliant. As the last day of the season approached they had a three point lead over Bayern. They had been on top for seven of the last eight weeks and were about to play lowly Unterhaching. All they needed was a draw to clinch the title.

Of course, life is never that easy for Leverkusen fans. After twenty minutes, new midfielder, Michael Ballack, scored an own goal and Leverkusen eventually lost 2:0. Bayern, meanwhile won their game and the championship. The scenes at Unterhaching after the game were terrible. Players sat slumped inconsolably on the pitch. Coach Christopher Daum hugged his young son, Michael Ballack gave a tearful interview before the cameras. The Bayer fans who had travelled to the game stayed in the ground, rooted to the spot, unable to understand how a team which had played such brilliant football all season could not be champions.

2001/2002 - Three missed opportunities

Two years later, the tragedy was even greater and led to Bayer being called Neverkusen in the English and Vizekusen in the German press.

Again Bayer had an absolutely brilliant season. They made a fantastic start and were unbeaten in their first 14 games, winning a series of 7 in a row at one point. They also reached the finals of the DFB Cup and the Champions League.

With three games to go, they had a five point lead and a massively superior goal difference over Dortmund, their nearest rivals. They then lost the next two games, while Dortmund won theirs. So they entered the last day of the season one point behind Dortmund. All was not lost, however. A win against Hertha Berlin could still secure the title if Dortmund failed to beat Werder Bremen, who were battling for a Champions League place.

Of course, things did not go to plan. Bayer beat Hertha, but Dortmund beat Bremen. The title had slipped away on the last day of the season again. But fans remained optimistic. There were still two finals to come - two more chances to win a trophy.

The first came a week later - the DFB Cup Final against Schalke 04. Despite taking an early lead and dominating the early stages of the game, Bayer eventually lost 4:1.

And the agony continued in the Champions League final against Real Madrid in Glasgow. A battling and passionate Bayer went down 2:1.

2002 to 2015 - Doing well but still chasing trophies

Bayer narrowly avoided relegation in 2002/03, but then finished third the next year, qualifying for the Champions League the following season. This was the start of a relatively successful era.

The club ended the next ten seasons consistently in the top third of the table and qualified for the Champions League three times and the Europa League four times.

A totally refurbished stadium which could take in more spectators and sound financial management led to stability on and off the pitch.

However, trophies continued to elude the club, and the Leverkusen jinx remained.

The 2008/09 season ended in classic Bayer Leverkusen style as the club narrowly lost the DFB Cup final to Werder Bremen.

In the 2009/10 season, despite at one stage achieving a run of 24 games without a defeat, the club only finished in 4th place.

Bayer finished second in 2010/11, achieved a top 5 place and competed in the Champions League or Europa League every year since then.

2016/2017 - Turbulence, change and disappointment

Leverkusen fans approached the start of 2016/17 with high hopes. In Roger Schmidt they had one of Germany's most innovative coaches and the club had become renowned for exciting, high octane football. A third place finish the previous season guaranteed a place in the Champions League for the fifth time in 6th successive seasons.

The club had held onto star striker Chicharito and had spent 57 million euros on new signings, including Julian Baumgartlinger and Kevin Volland.

After a reasonable start, results started to go against the Werkself. By March the club had lost 11 out of 23 games, including a 6:2 thrashing at the hands of Borussia Dortmund. The highlight of the Champions League campaign was a win against Spurs at Wembley, but Leverkusen were knocked out of the round of 16 by Atletico Madrid.

The Leverkusen board decided to part company with Schmidt and took on former Turkish international, Tayfun Korkut.

This change at the top did little to correct Leverkusen's downward drift. One win, four draws and five defeats led to Korkut's dismissal after 10 games.

Leverkusen finished the season in 12th place.

2017/2018 - The return of Heiko Herrlich

In June, the club announced that Heiko Herrlich would take over as coach. Herrlich began his Bundesliga career at Leverkusen before moving to Borussia Mönchengladbach and Borussia Dortmund. As a manager, he led Jahn Regensburg from the fourth to the second division in less than two years. He had also been coach at Bochum and Unterhaching.

The new season began well for the Werkself and a 12 match unbeaten run led many fans to dream of qualification for next the season's Champions League. Unfortunately Bayer's campaign faltered in the second half of the season. They came agonisingly close to a Champions League spot, but finished behind Hoffenheim and Dortmund on goal difference.

2018/2019 - Another change of coach

A 4th place finish in the league secured a return of Champions League football to the BayArena. The club also enjoyed relative success in other competitions, getting as far as the round of 16 in the cup and the Round of 32 in the Europa League.

Heiko Herrlich left the club in December and was replaced by Peter Bosz.

2019/2020 - Still in Europe and a good cup run

Bayer dropped out of the Champions League in the group stage but progressed to the quarter-finals of the Europa League. They were runners-up in the cup and came 5th in the league.

2020/2021 - Inconsistent performances

A 2:1 defeat to 3. Liga Rot Weiss Essen eliminated Leverkusen from the DFB Cup in the quarter-finals.

The Werkself stormed through the group stage of the Europa League, winning five games. But lost to Young Boys Bern in the first knockout round.

By the halfway stage, Leverkusen were in 3rd place in the Bundesliga and on track to secure a Champions League place for the following season.

Performances were less consistent in the second half of the season but still good enough to secure 6th place and Europa League qualification.

Peter Bosz was dismissed in March and temporarily replaced by Hannes Wolf. Gerardo Seoane was then appointed coach in July 2021.

2021/22 - Improvements in all areas

Bayer entertained fans with some scintillating attacking football from the start of the season.

Florian Wirtz and Patrik Schick emerged as a highly potent partnership. After seven games Bayer were jostling for the top spot with reigning champions Bayern. Once again, the Munich side pulled away from the leading pack and comfortably won the league. But despite losing Wirtz to injury for many of the final games, the Werkself finished the season in third place

Bayer progressed to the knockout stage of the Europa League, losing only one of the group matches. They were knocked out of the round of sixteen by Atalanta Bergamo.

Kaiserslautern knocked Bayer out of the DFB Cup in the second round.

4

STORIES

Tradition and history are vital elements of football culture. Every club has stories to tell. Here are some of the best known about Bayer Leverkusen.

Bayer's two 'ghost' goals

1. Stefan Kießling and Hoffenheim

The Germans use the word 'Phantomtor' or 'ghost goal' to describe a goal that wasn't really a goal - for example, because the ball didn't cross the line.

The most recent ghost goal for Bayer happened on Friday 18 October 2013. Bayer, playing Hoffenheim away, were 1:0 up halfway through the second half. A Bayer corner came in from the left and veteran striker Stefan Kießling headed the ball into the side netting. He then turned away, head in hands in disappointment.

What happened next was bizarre, to say the least. Somehow, the ball had got through the side netting. Seeing the Hoffenheim keeper picking the ball out of the goal, Kießling's teammates began cheering, and the referee gave a goal.

Replays show clearly that the ball struck the side netting and then squeezed through a gap into the goal. Kießling's body language showed that he knew it wasn't a goal, but he didn't clarify the situation. Indeed, one German tabloid, Bild, hired a lip reader to analyse video footage of the incident. The paper claimed that the press officer advised him to maintain he didn't see what happened. But the goal and the final outcome of the match both stood. Of course, Hoffenheim fans will remember the incident and the culprits - referee Felix Brych and Stefan Kießling - for a very long time. And there is little doubt that the ghost goal at Hoffenheim contributed to the decision to introduce goal line technology at Bundesliga games in the 2015/16 season.

2. Arne-Larsen Økland and Bayern München

The Hoffenheim incident was not the first involving a dubious goal for Bayer.

On 7 March 1981, Bayer were playing Bayern Munich at home. Norwegian Arne-Larsen Økland scored a hat trick in the first half, scoring goals in the 4th 14th and 19th minutes and Bayer emerged 3:0 winners. But the game, and probably Økland himself, are probably better remembered for an incident in the second half.

In the 71st minute, Økland, who had tormented the Bayern defence throughout the match, let off a shot which hit the support behind the goal. The ball then squeezed through a hole in the side netting into the Bayern goal. Although the

Leverkusen players seemed a bit confused about what had happened, the referee was in no doubt - it was a goal!

This decision led to chaotic scenes as the Bayern players and officials protested energetically. The referee then consulted his linesman before confirming his original decision.

Slowly, the protests of the Bayern players died down, and the ball was returned to the centre spot for kick-off. At this point Arne-Larsen Økland approached the referee and said : "That was not a goal." The referee picked up the ball, ran back to the Bayern goal and placed it on the edge of the six-yard box, indicating a goal kick.

When asked about the incident later Økland said: "I had to tell the referee." But when asked if he would have done the same if Bayer had not been ahead, he only smiled. [6]

Bayer's greatest triumph - 1987/88 UEFA Cup Winners

Bayer started this campaign as clear favourites to beat Austria Vienna in the first game. No German team had ever lost to an Austrian one in this competition. Of course, things did not go to plan. The first game, played in Vienna, ended goalless, and at halftime in the second leg the score stood at 1:1. Fortunately for their long suffering fans, Bayer went up a gear in the second half and ended 5:1 winners.

Next up were Toulouse, who had finished third in France the previous season and had several well-known names in their squad. The first leg, played in France, ended in a hard-fought 1:1 draw. Although a 0:0 draw in the home leg would have been enough for Bayer to progress, the game ended 1:0.

For the first time in the club's history, Bayer had reached the final stages of a European competition. Their opponents were the mighty Feyenoord Rotterdam - 12 times Dutch champions, and previous winners of the UEFA Cup. The first leg was again played away, and after 30 minutes Bayer found themselves 2:0 ahead. Goalkeeping errors by the usually totally reliable Rüdiger Vollborn allowed the Dutchmen to get back into the game, which ended 2:2. Bayer then won the home leg 1:0 and progressed to the quarterfinal.

This time, the opponents were none other than Barcelona, one of the best known and most successful clubs on the planet. The first leg, played at home, ended 0:0. The second game was played in front of 120,000 spectators at the famous Nou Camp stadium. After going ahead halfway through the second half, thanks to a goal from Tita, the Bayer team heroically resisted wave after wave of Barcelona attacks to emerge as 1:0 winners.

The semi-final was an all-German affair as Bayer were drawn against Werder Bremen. This was the team Bayer had wanted to avoid as Bremen were Germany's 'in form' team and well on the way to winning the Bundesliga.

The first leg was played at home in front of a disappointingly small crowd of 15,000, and Bayer won 1:0 thanks to a goal from Alois Reinhardt. In the second leg, cheered on by a big and noisy crowd, Bremen applied massive pressure from the start. But a superb defensive performance from the entire Bayer team kept them out. The game ended 0:0 and Bayer were in the final.

By one of those strange coincidences that football produces, their opponents were to be the other Barcelona team -

Español. Bayer made a decent start to the first game, played in the Estadi de Sarrià in front of 40,000 spectators, but went behind just before halftime. Two further goals in the first ten minutes of the second half gave the Spaniards a 3:0 lead, which is how the game ended. Players and fans were devastated. It was Bayer's first loss for 14 successive European games. And such a heavy loss seemed to have put the cup almost beyond reach.

The Ulrich Haberland Stadion was completely sold out for the second leg. The Leverkuseners hoped that an early goal would get the crowd behind them and make the Spanish team nervous. But they just couldn't score - and when they finally did get the ball in the net, the referee disallowed the goal. So at the break it was 0:0.

Then, in the 57th minute, Tita broke the logjam and scored.

A short while later, Falko Götz scored a second. Was there enough time to score a third? With 9 minutes still on the clock, Bum-Kun Cha did just that. Incredibly, Bayer had got back onto even terms with Español.

There were no more goals in normal or extra time, so penalties would finally decide the result. And after many twists and turns and another heroic performance from keeper Vollborn, Bayer emerged 3:2 winners. They had won their first ever major title!

Bayer's first national trophy - and a bitter aftertaste.

In 1993, Bayer 04 Leverkusen won its very first national trophy, the German cup.

The journey to the final was far from straightforward and the long-suffering fans were forced to sweat on more than one occasion.

In the second round, a lacklustre performance meant they only just beat a very defensive minded 1. FC Kaiserslautern with an 84th minute penalty.

They struggled to beat fourth tier VfR Heilbronn in the next round, only winning courtesy of two very lucky second half goals.

Next, they were drawn to play at home against second division Hertha Berlin and again Bayer made their fans suffer and only went through thanks to an 83rd minute goal from substitute Andreas Thom.

The quarter final was also against 2. Bundesliga opposition in the form of FC Carl Zeiss Jena. This time, two goals from Andreas Thom gave Bayer a comfortable 2:0 victory and a place in the semi-finals.

They were drawn against Eintracht Frankfurt, whose manager, Dragoslav Stepanovic, was negotiating to become the next Bayer manager. Leverkusen comfortably won 3:0.

Ironically, this hastened the departure of manager Reinhard Saftig, the architect of the club's best ever cup run. Stepanovic announced his resignation immediately after the match and by taking him as 'adviser' Bayer were able to bring forward his appointment. This victory over Frankfurt must have been a particularly bitter pill for Saftig as the manager on the touchline for the final was Stepanovic - the losing manager of the semi-final.

The final was against Hertha Berlin - but not the professional 2. Bundesliga team that Bayer had knocked out in the third round. In Germany, professional clubs are allowed to field a team of amateur players in the lower leagues, and so it was against this Hertha team that Bayer were to play the final. To get there, the Berlin amateurs had seen off top teams 1. FC Nürnberg and title holders Hannover 96, as well as 2. Bundesliga outfits VfB Leipzig and Chemnitzer FC.

So the Hertha players started the final brimming with confidence. The game was played in Berlin and must have felt like a home game to them. As clear underdogs, the Berliners had the support of the entire nation (apart from Bayer fans, of course), and throughout the game a very partisan crowd cheered wildly every time Hertha got the ball, and booed and whistled raucously when Leverkusen had possession.

Bayer dominated a goalless first half, and the longer the game went on, the more nervous their players must have felt. The winning goal came from an error by the Hertha goalkeeper, who until then had put in a flawless performance. In the 77th minute, he was only able to parry a hard shot from Franco Foda. Pavel Hapal collected the ball and sent it towards the right-hand side of goal. Ulf Kirsten then beat his man to head home and score the only goal of the final.

Unfortunately, the moment of Bayer's greatest triumph was soured by the reaction of the Berlin crowd and the national media, who were disappointed that the underdog had lost and they had not been party to a stunning upset. Many spectators booed and whistled as the Bayer players went to collect the trophy and as they did a lap of honour. Bayer fans watching at home didn't even get to see their team on the victors' podium as the TV station ended the broadcast early. Celebrations only really started in earnest back at the hotel.

Leverkusen fans and the Bayer Cross

The A3 motorway is the second longest motorway in Germany. It goes all the way from North Rhine-Westfalia in the northwest to Bavaria in the south. The journey along the first stretch of its 778 kilometres is pretty dull. That is until you pass Leverkusen, where you will see the famous Bayer Cross. This vast construction depicting the Bayer logo was first built in 1933. It was 120 meters high and 50 meters wide. At night it was lit by 1,710 lightbulbs and could be seen from 5 kilometres. Removed in 1944 but then rebuilt in 1958, it has guided Leverkuseners home for over a century and is, for many, a symbol of the city. In 2007 the company decided it was time to remove this monument, but Bayer 04 fans led a remarkable action to save it. They ran a highly effective media campaign and gathered a 20,000 signature petition. The firm changed its mind. The Bayer Cross has been brought up to date and the 1,710 lightbulbs have been replaced by diodes that use 80% less energy.[9]

The original Ultras

"Ultras" are a football club's most active and passionate fans. They are the ones behind the goal who sing and chant for 90 minutes and more every week. They organise the amazing displays you see at German clubs. Nowadays, Ultras are a vital part of every club's tradition and culture. And Bayer Leverkusen has one of the oldest Ultra groups in the country. The Soccer Boyz was founded in 1989, when Ultras groups were unheard of in most German clubs.

There are currently over 270 registered fan clubs with about 25,000 members.

The original fan project

Almost all top German clubs now have a 'Fanprojekt'. These are initiatives that bring club and fans together. They support community development, help combat racism or hooliganism, provide a focus for youth work and encourage communication between fans, club and police. Nowadays, in recognition of their positive impact, they receive funding from their clubs, the football authorities (DFB) and the government.

This was not always the case. Funding and support from the DFB only came about because of energetic lobbying by a small group of clubs, including Borussia Mönchengladbach, Hannover 96 and Bayer 04 Leverkusen. These clubs were already convinced of the advantages of working with fans in this way and thanks to their efforts and persuasion, the initiative has spread across the country and funding is now provided.

Leverkusen - the birthplace of aspirin, heroin and polyurethane

Although not discovered by Bayer, the company developed and manufactured aspirin from 1897 and initially owned the name. The employee who led the development of aspirin was called Felix Hoffmann, who was a member of a research team led by Heinrich Dreser. As well as aspirin, this team also invented another new pain-killer, which they called heroin. For a time, Bayer also manufactured and sold this. When side-effects, including user dependency, came to light, Bayer stopped selling heroin. The company eventually also sold the rights to the name aspirin.

In later life, ill health forced Dreser to leave the firm, and he died of a stroke. According to rumours he had taken a daily dose of heroin in the years before his death. Had he taken the other wonder drug, he might well have lived longer.

Polyurethane is found just about everywhere in modern life. The chair you are sitting on, the bed you sleep in and the house you live in will probably all contain this solid foam. It was invented in 1937 by Professor Otto Bayer, the founder of the Bayer company.

Rudi Völler's Rant on Live TV

Fans of the English Premier League will remember Kevin Keegan's famous rant about Alex Ferguson in 1996.

At the time Keegan was manager of Newcastle United - like Bayer Leverkusen, a side with a history of letting major trophies slip from its grasp at the last minute.

Newcastle had made a fantastic start to the season, and in March were 12 points ahead of Manchester United. This lead gradually slipped away and they went into the end phase of the season one point behind.

Ferguson then played one of his famous mind games, suggesting Newcastle's next opponents might give them an easy ride.

Predictably, Keegan flipped and launched a tirade live on radio. Amongst other things, he said he would "love it if we beat them!"

Unfortunately for Keegan, Newcastle didn't win the Premiership, and have not come close to doing so since.[12]

Leverkusen's Director of Sport, Rudi Völler, had a similar moment in 2003 when he was managing the German national team.

They call it "Völlers Wutrede" (angry speech, rant) and it also happened on live TV.

Germany had just drawn a Euro 2004 qualifying match with outsiders Iceland. Völler was invited into the TV studio for an interview. Unfortunately, on his way there way he had overheard two well-known pundits, Günter Netzer and Gerhard Delling, making very disparaging comments about the team and its tactics.

Still feeling the emotions of the game and already stressed, Völler completely lost his temper. He complained about the media ("making judgements from your high horses"), and had particularly barbed comments to make about Netzer. "Günter (Netzer) played shit in the past. They played stationary football!"

This incident is one of the most famous in Bundesliga TV history. There is a fascinating recording of the incident, which shows how Völler starts quietly but then gets more and more worked up.

Bayer Leverkusen is not a plastic club

German football fans are rightly proud of the 50 + 1 rule, which makes sure clubs cannot fall into the hands of one owner.

They are scornful of so called 'plastic' clubs that have sprung up with the backing of wealthy individuals or big companies. They worry that clubs like RB Leipzig (created and owned by Red Bull) are distorting the game and will one day be able to buy themselves success at the expense of clubs owned by and run for their fans.

The situation with Bayer Leverkusen is complicated. The club has a relatively small fan base and is sponsored by the pharmaceutical giant Bayer AG. But it would be grossly unfair to give Leverkusen the same label as Leipzig.

The club was founded over 110 years ago by Bayer employees, and has always had a very close relationship with the company and the town. Although it is still strongly associated with the concern, it is neither owned nor run by Bayer, which does not pay in nearly as much as, for example, VW does at Wolfsburg.

Bayer Leverkusen would maintain that its successes both on and off the pitch are the result of sound financial management, imaginative and innovative business plans, shrewd player acquisitions through the transfer market, an excellent youth system and good coaching.

To accusations that the club lacks tradition, the fans will point out that the club has 110 years of history, that the first group of Ultras in Germany emerged from Bayer, and that the club was one of the first to support fan liaison projects.

The club and its fans are sensitive to the charge that they have moved away from their working-class roots. They point out that Leverkusen tries very hard to be a very welcoming and family-friendly club and that this can sometimes soften the atmosphere in the ground. They argue that this does not mean their passion is any less, and that it is good business to make grounds safe and welcoming places. The children who come today with their parents are likely to be the fans of tomorrow.

5

FAMOUS NAMES

Willibert Kremer

Willibert Kremer was the manager who led Bayer 04 Leverkusen into the promised land of the Bundesliga. He also converted the club into a modern, professional organisation able to compete and flourish at the top level.

He nearly didn't go to Bayer at all. He had been a player with MSV Duisburg since 1966. When he finished playing in 1971 he was taken on by the club to manage the youth team and then in 1973 was appointed as head coach. At this time Duisburg were one of Germany's top teams, with international stars like Ronnie Worms and Rudi Seliger in their squad. Disappointed that the club was making no effort to renew his contract when it ran out, he resigned in March 1976. He told the press at the time: "I don't need to go down on my knees and beg for a job."

Initially Kremer planned to take a year out, but Bayer Leverkusen were really keen to take him on and basically pestered him until he agreed to come.

He arrived at a club at serious risk of relegation. His first training session was a revelation to him, when several players couldn't keep up with a warmup that was standard in the Bundesliga. Fortunately, he was able to improve the team enough to secure second division status.

Kremer discovered he had joined a club beset by outdated practices and his subsequent success was down to his determination to make the club more professional at every level. He also worked tirelessly to improve the facilities, equipment and training made available to the youth team, making sure that talented youngsters made Bayer their first choice rather than neighbours 1. FC Köln.

He became a jack-of-all-trades - spotting talent, negotiating with parents, checking up on grounds maintenance. He was relentless in his drive to improve all aspects of the club, not even taking a holiday for his first few years in charge.

His stubbornness, attention to detail and persistence eventually paid off. Three years later Bayer were in the Bundesliga. In their last year in the 2. Bundesliga, the club secured promotion three games before the end of a fantastic season. They accumulated a record total of 59 points and scored 87 goals while only conceding 34. In the game that made promotion certain, Bayer came back from 3:0 in the last 20 minutes to achieve a 3:3 draw against Uerdingen.

Kremer stayed with Bayer for another two years before moving on to 1860 München, but the circumstances of his departure were disappointing for him. During his time at

Bayer, he had turned down approaches by several top clubs, and when, in 1981, 1. FC Nürnberg offered him a job, he asked to be released. The management at Bayer turned him down and warned Nürnberg off. His disappointment at missing out on a move to such a big club doubled when, two months later, Bayer dismissed him.

He had a long managerial career, finally retiring in 1995, and he eventually made his peace with his former club. When Bayer won the UEFA Cup in 1988, the club recognised his contributions to its transformation into a member of the elite of European football.

He now works as a scout for Bayer 04 Leverkusen.

Career highlights

As a player

1961 - 1962 — Borussia Mönchengladbach

1962 - 1964 — Viktoria Köln

1964 - 1966 — Hertha Berlin

1966 - 1971 — MSV Duisburg

As a manager

1973 - 1976 — MSV Duisburg

1976 - 1981 — Bayer 04 Leverkusen

1982 - 1860 — München

1982 - 1985 — Fortuna Düsseldrorf

1985 - 1986 — Eintracht Braunschweig

1989 - 1992 — MSV Duisburg

1992 - 1993 — Tennis Borussia Berlin

1994 - 1995 — Tennis Borussia Berlin

∿

Dettmar Cramer

Dettmar Cramer had two nicknames. Some called him 'The Football Professor' because of his attention to detail. Others called him "Napoleon" because of his stature.

He played football for Viktoria Dortmund and Germania Wiesbaden, but he is best known in Germany and beyond as a football manager.

Cramer began his coaching career with Teutonia Lippstadt and FC Paderborn, but the legendary Sepp Herberger spotted his potential as a trainer and invited Cramer to join the DFB. He was subsequently appointed Head Coach for Western Germany.

He then managed the Japanese national side ahead of the 1960 Olympics before returning to Germany in 1964, when he and Udo Lattek worked as assistants to Helmut Schön with the national team. From 1967 to 1974, he fulfilled several international roles for FIFA and was head coach of the USA team.

In 1975, he took over as manager of FC Bayern Munich. After a shaky start, during which his management style was strongly criticised, he led Bayern to victory in the 1975 and 1976 European Cup. A disappointing season in 1976/77 led to him resigning his position and moving to Eintracht Frankfurt. He could not improve Frankfurt's performance and eventually left the club in 1978.

Then, at the very end of the 1981/82 season, he came to the rescue at Bayer 04 Leverkusen.

The 1981/82 season had been a miserable one for Bayer 04. A disappointing start left the club 14th in the table, one point above the relegation zone with three games to play before the winter break. Then came the dismissal on 22 November of longstanding manager Willibert Kremer, who had led Bayer into the Bundesliga two years previously. His assistant, Gerd Kentschke, was appointed interim manager and Bayer ended the first half of the season with two draws and a defeat.

Things did not improve after the winter break and Bayer ended the season third from bottom, having conceded 72 goals and accumulated a miserly 25 points. Fortunately for Bayer 04, this was the first year of the relegation play-offs, where the third from bottom of the 1. Bundesliga play two games against the third from top of the 2 Bundesliga. To keep top tier status, they needed to defeat Kickers Offenbach.

Four days before the first match, Bayer appointed a new coach Dettmar Cramer was able to instil in the team enough confidence and mental strength to win both games and hang onto their place in the Bundesliga. Once this was secured, Cramer set about building on the work of his predecessor to make the club more professional. Under his leadership, players began to be employed by the club directly rather than by Bayer. He engaged a PR expert to improve the club's image. The coach and his team visited fan groups to answer questions. His charisma, calm and charm undoubtedly attracted new fans to the club.

In his second season at Bayer, he led them to a 9th place finish in the Bundesliga - the best so far. Unfortunately, his team did not build on this success the next year and he was dismissed in 1985. His legacy was a confident, professional football club.

After leaving, Bayer Cramer worked as a coach with various international clubs and then retired in 2002.

He died in 2015, aged 90.

~

Christoph Daum

Christoph Daum played football for Eintracht Duisburg and 1. FC Köln, but it was as a coach that he made his reputation.

He began his coaching career in 1981 with the 1. FC Köln reserve team. In 1985, he became assistant coach to the senior team and a year later moved to the top position.

Daum was a highly innovative coach. He was very interested in sports science and psychology, and was extremely good at motivating his players. He was also witty, charismatic and very media friendly.

He moved to VfB Stuttgart in 1990 and won the German Championships in 1991/92. The next season he made a mistake in the first round of the European Cup by putting forward a fourth foreign player when the rules only allowed three. UEFA ruled that the game should be replayed. Leeds won, Stuttgart went out of the competition and Daum was sacked.

His next position was with Besiktas in Turkey. He won the Turkish cup in 1994 and the Turkish league in 1995, but was sacked in 1996.

Two years later, Daum returned to Germany to coach Bayer Leverkusen. He achieved three second-place finishes in the four seasons he was at the club and was tipped to become the next German national team manager. At about this time, rumours surfaced in the press that Daum had used cocaine. To clear his name, he submitted hair samples to the authorities for analysis. Unfortunately for Daum, they showed he was indeed a cocaine user. Facing the prospect of a prison sentence, Daum eventually admitted that he had used the drug. He was fired by Leverkusen and, of course, the DFB did not offer him the job of national team coach.

Unable to find work in Germany, he moved abroad, working initially with former team Besiktas, then Austria Wien, with whom he won the Austrian Championship.

In 2003, he switched to Turkish side Fenerbahce, who won the Turkish league twice under his leadership. At the end of his third season Fenerbahce narrowly lost the championship to rivals Galatasaray and Daum resigned.

In 2006, Daum was appointed manager of 1. FC Köln. Under his leadership, the team gained promotion back in to the Bundesliga in 2008. He left the club in 2009.

In 2009, Daum began a second stretch at Fenerbahce. Unfortunately, success eluded him this time, and in 2010 he and the club agreed to go separate ways.

In March 2011, Daum was appointed coach at Eintracht Frankfurt to replace Michael Skibbe, who had been sacked following a decline in results. Daum could not arrest this decline. 3 draws and 4 defeats in the 7 games he was in charge was not enough to stave off relegation and Frankfurt were relegated in May. Daum then left the club.

After a 6 month break, Daum took over at Club Brugge in Belgium. He led the club to a 2nd place finish to the 2011/12 season but then resigned for family reasons.

Daum's final coaching position was at Bursaspor, where he worked from 14 August 2013 to 24 March 2014.

Honours

VfB Stuttgart

Bundesliga: 1992

DFL-Supercup: 1992

Beşiktaş

Süper Lig: 1995

Turkish Cup: 1994

Austria Wien

Austrian Football Bundesliga: 2003

Fenerbahçe

Süper Lig: 2004, 2005

Turkish Super Cup: 2009

∼

Reiner Calmund

The story of Bayer 04 Leverkusen would not be complete without a section on Reiner Calmund, who between 1976 and 2004 was ever present at the club and who influenced its development both on and off the pitch.

He started as a youth worker and stadium announcer. By 1988, he was manager of the professional football section of the club and in 1999, he was appointed director of Bayer 04 Leverkusen Fußball Limited.

Calmund attracted a series of stars to the club, including Bernd Schuster, Ulf Kirsten, Michael Ballack and Rudi Völler. He used all his persuasive skills to make sure that Leverkusen was the first Bundesliga team to recruit players from the former East Germany. He also brought exciting Brazilian stars such as Jorginho, Emerson and Lúcio to Germany. He was a big man with an even bigger personality who contributed massively to the club's progress into the elite of European football.

In 2004, Calmund announced he was resigning for health reasons. He was replaced by his deputy, Wolfgang Holzhäuser.

Two years later, it emerged that the club had actually fired him. He had made an unauthorised payment of 58,0000 euros to a football agent called Volker Graul to secure the first option to buy two Croatian players. Although the club had been interested in the players, no transfers took place and there was no paperwork to go with the deal.

Why Calmund made this payment, why he kept it from the club, why the club remained silent for two years about the affair and what happened to the money is still unclear. Calmund was adamant that Holzhäuser knew about the payment, but the man hotly denied this himself. The club explained that Calmund was allowed to leave in the way he did because of all the things he had done for Bayer 04 Leverkusen over such a long period. Officials felt that it was right to grant him a dignified departure.

What happened to the money also remains unclear. Graul claimed to have passed it on to two agents from the former Yugoslavia. One of them has since died and the other denies receiving any money.

People thought that the truth might emerge when the authorities charged Calmund with embezzlement. However, these charges were dropped after he paid a fine of 30,000 and so the true story behind the Calmund affair remains a mystery.

∼

Ulf Kirsten

Ulf Kirsten was born in the former German Democratic Republic and played for the GDR national team. After German reunification, he played for the German national team.

He began his playing career with Dynamo Dresden in 1983, making 154 appearances and scoring 57 goals. He was East German footballer of the year 1998/90.

He was then one of the first East German footballers to join the Bundesliga after German reunification in 1989. He joined Bayer 04 Leverkusen in 1993, making 350 appearances, the second highest of any player. In this time he scored 182 goals, becoming the highest goal scorer ever for the club (His nearest rival, Herbert Waas only scored 72). He stayed with Bayer for the rest of his career.

He played 49 times for East Germany and 51 times for the post re-unification German team and scored 35 international goals.

He was strong, fairly short and with a low centre of gravity. This enabled him to shield the ball particularly well. Many have compared his playing style to that of Gerd Müller.

Kirsten was also famous for his unshaven appearance and quick growing beard. Shaver manufacturer Braun used him to advertise their products, and for a time he used to shave at the side of the pitch at half time.

Honours

With Dynamo Dresden

DDR Championship: 1989, 1990

DDR Cup: 1985, 1990

With Bayer 04 Leverkusen

DFB Cup — 1992/93

∾

Rüdiger Vollborn

Every club has a super-loyal player, supporter or worker who has devoted his entire career to the club. That's what

Rüdiger Vollborn is. Although born in Berlin, he kept goal for Bayer 04 Leverkusen for his entire professional career, making a total of 401 appearances.

He was a vital member of the team that won the 1988 UEFA Cup and played a pivotal role in the final. He was also a member of the DFB Cup-winning team of 1993.

At the end of his playing career, he worked for 12 years as goal-keeping coach at Bayer - initially with the youth team and from 2003 with the first team. Over this time, he spotted and developed a stream of great keepers. His most famous protege was René Adler, who joined Bayer 04 as a 15-year-old in 2000. Vollborn didn't just look after the youngster professionally for the next four years. He also took Adler into his own home and family. He and his wife became second parents to the budding star at this crucial stage in his development.

Although he David Thiel replaced him as goal-keeping coach in 2011, he still works for the club, as chief fan liaison officer.

$\sim$

Andreas Thom

Andreas Thom was the first player from the former East Germany to sign for a West German club.

He began his professional career at Dynamo Berlin, with whom he won the East German Championship six times and the East German Cup twice. In 1988, he was the top scorer in East Germany. He played for the East German national team 51 times.

In 1989, only weeks after the fall of the Berlin Wall, he became the first East German player to sign for a Bundesliga club when he joined Bayer for a transfer fee of 2.5 million marks. He was also one of the highest paid players in the league, earning 12,000 marks per week.

The story of his arrival in Leverkusen is interesting. The last game before the winter break should have taken place against FC 08 Homburg on 12 December 1989. Club business manager, Reiner Calmund, requested a postponement until the spring, claiming that the pitch was unplayable. Crowds still came to the stadium on the day - but not to see a football match. Instead, they and the assembled media were presented with a new star - Andreas Thorn. He was flown over from Berlin, where the last details of his transfer had literally just been agreed, and presented to fans and the press, given a tour of his new home, before returning to Berlin to bid farewell to friends and teammates. He scored his first goal for the club in his first match and went on to make 161 appearances and score 36 goals.

After five years at Leverkusen, during which he helped win the German Cup in 1993, Glasgow Celtic signed him for £2.2 million. This was a club record at the time.

Not long after he arrived, the Scottish press asked Thom how he felt about the animosity of the Old Firm derbies. He said that playing for his first club, Dynamo Berlin, had prepared him well. Dynamo Berlin were controlled by the Stasi, the hated and feared East German secret police. Everybody knew this, and in a country with few opportunities for free expression, booing and jeering the Stasi team was a relatively safe way to say what you felt about the government. So as a Dynamo Berlin player, Thom got used to constant hostility from the fans of other clubs. This was to prove to be an excellent grounding for the febrile atmosphere of Glasgow football.

In 1998, he returned to Germany, spending the last four years of his career with Hertha Berlin.

On retiring as a player, he stayed with Hertha Berlin for four years as assistant coach. After a two-year spell as assistant coach with Holstein Kiel, he returned to Hertha in 2010.

Honours

Club

Dynamo Berlin

East German Championship: 1984, 1985, 1986, 1987, 1988

East German Cup: 1988, 1989

Bayer 04 Leverkusen

German Cup: 1993

Glasgow Celtic

Scottish League champions: 1998

Scottish League Cup: 1997

International

UEFA European Championship: Runner-up 1992

Individual Honours

East German Footballer of the Year: 1988

Bernd Schuster

His nickname was 'der blonde Engel' - the blond angel. He was physically very strong, skilful on the ball and had a powerful shot. He was undoubtedly one of the best midfield players of his day in the world, played football at the highest level for 20 years and achieved many honours at both club and national level.

Unfortunately, his 'difficult' character repeatedly caused him problems at all the clubs he played for and made some managers reluctant to take him on.

He played for Bayer 04 Leverkusen for three seasons, making 59 appearances, scoring 8 goals (including the 3 best Bundesliga goals of 1994)

At the end of his playing career, he became a manager and has worked for 9 different clubs.

Schuster first came to prominence at 18 when he put in some superb performances for the German under-19 side. He was so impressive that German champions 1. FC Köln, at the time led by the legendary Hennes Weisweiler, plucked him from the youth team of his home club Augsburg.

Although the tradition in Germany at the time was to protect young players and develop them slowly, Schuster was so good that he was playing for the Köln first team before he was 19.

By 1980, he was playing for the German national side and his performances at Euro 80 - particularly in the final - brought him to the attention of the wider world.

The next season, he signed for Barcelona and he was to be a mainstay of the Catalan club for most of the 1980s. His partnership with Diego Maradona is still considered in Spain to have been one of the best combinations ever.

Next came a highly controversial move, in 1988, to arch rivals Real Madrid. Two years later, he signed for Atletico Madrid.

Schuster was enticed back to Germany to join Bayer 04 Leverkusen in 1993. This was not the first time Bayer had tried to sign the gifted player. Negotiations were broken off on two previous occasions because the Leverkusen coaches of the day felt unable to work with him or feared the disruptive influence he would have on the squad.

He left Bayer after three seasons and ended his playing career in Mexico.

He began his managerial career with Fortuna Köln in 1997, before moving across town to 1. FC Köln the following season. Since then he has managed teams in Spain (including Real Madrid), Turkey and Ukraine.

Schuster was, by all accounts, a very difficult personality to manage. Here are a few examples :

At 1 FC Köln, he fell out with manager Karl-Heinz Heddergott, calling him an amateur.

Jupp Derval excluded him from the German squad because of perceived rudeness to a fellow player.

In 1984, he refused to travel to Albania with the national team because he wanted to be present at the birth of his child. The ensuing public criticism caused him to decide to retire completely from international football. Even the great

Franz Beckenbauer could not persuade him to change his mind.

When he was substituted in the 1986 European Cup Final, he stormed out of the stadium in a blind rage.

In 1988, he was part of the Barcelona 'mutiny' - a group of players calling publicly for the resignation of club president Josep Lluís Núñez.

In 1993 Schuster was one of a group of 5 Atletico Madrid players who surrounded the referee at the end of the UEFA Cup final to accuse him of corruption. This earned him a 5 game ban.

His time at Leverkusen was stormy. According to Uli Hesse, he arrived with "5 fighting dogs, 10 bodyguards and 15 horses". Although he initially handled himself well, things went from bad to worse in the 1995/96 season and he actually came to blows with manager Ribbeck. His behaviour led to him being banned from the squad, but Schuster successfully won an injunction which forced the club to let him train with them.

Honours

Club

FC Barcelona

La Liga: 1985

Copa del Rey: 1981, 1983, 1988

European Cup Winners' Cup: 1981–82

Supercopa de España: 1983

Copa de la Liga: 1983, 1986

European Cup Runner-up: 1986

Real Madrid

La Liga: 1989, 1990

Copa del Rey: 1989

Supercopa de España: 1989

Atlético Madrid

La Liga Runner-up: 1991

Copa del Rey: 1991, 1992

International

West Germany

UEFA European Football Championship: 1980

Individual honours

UEFA Euro Team of the Tournament: 1980

Ballon d'Or Runner-up: 1980

Ballon d'Or Third Place: 1981 and 1985

La Liga: Don Balón Award for Best Foreign Player 1985, 1991

Coach

Getafe

Copa del Rey Runner-up: 2007

Real Madrid

La Liga: 2008

Supercopa de España: 2008[23]

Bernd Schneider

Bernd Schneider was renowned for his dribbling, passing and technique. Although he was primarily a midfielder, he could also play on both wings. His skill with the ball earned him the nickname "Der weiße Brasilianer" (the white Brazilian)

He had a phenomenal work rate which, along with his loyalty and commitment to the club, made him a great favourite with the fans.

He played for Bayer Leverkusen for ten years, scoring 39 goals.

Schneider began his football career with his local home side Carl Zeiss Jena in the former German Democratic Republic. He then moved to the Bundesliga to join Eintracht Frankfurt, before signing for Bayer Leverkusen in 1999. He was a key player in the side which achieved second place in the Bundesliga in 2000 and 2002. He appeared in 19 of the games Bayer played on their way to the 2002 Champions League Final and played in the 2002 DFB Cup final. By 2009 Schneider had begun to suffer a series of injuries and he retired later that year. His farewell game was an exhibition match between an all-stars team led by Schneider and the Bayer Leverkusen team. 20,000 fans turned out to watch him one last time.

Schneider first played for Germany in 1999, when he played in two games during the Confederations Cup.

He quickly established himself as a key squad member who was appreciated for his versatility. He was a member of the German squad in the 2002 World Cup, the 2004 European Championship and the 2006 World Cup and formed a formidable partnership with Ballack, Schweinsteiger and Frings.

He played 81 games for Germany and scored four goals.

After retiring, he worked as a scout for Bayer Leverkusen

Honours

Club

Bayer Leverkusen

Bundesliga Runner-up: 2000, 2002

DFB-Pokal: Runner-up: 2002, 2009

UEFA Champions League Runner-up: 20062

International

FIFA World Cup Runner-up: 2002, 3rd Place 2006

FIFA Confederations Cup 3rd Place: 2005

$\sim$

Michael Ballack

Michael Ballack was one of the greatest and most versatile footballers of his generation and is among the top German national goal scorers ever. He was a superb passer of the ball, was extremely strong and had a powerful shot. He could play with either foot.

Pele included him in his list of FIFA's Greatest Living Players and nominated him UEFA Club Midfielder of the year 2002. He was German Footballer of the Year in 2002, 2003 and 2005.

Ballack played for elite teams in the German Bundesliga and the English Premier League, winning national and international trophies at club and international level.

He had two spells at Bayer Leverkusen - from 1999 to 2002 and from 2010 to 2012.

He began to play football when he was 7. His father, who had been a second division player himself, sent him first to his local team and then, when the family moved, to FS Karl-Marx Stadt (to be renamed Chemnitzer FC).

His reputation with the youth team as a solid midfielder earned him the nickname 'the little Kaiser' - a reference to Franz Beckenbauer. In 1995, Chemnitz offered him a professional contract and he played his first game on 4 August.

The young Ballack made 14 appearances that season for Chemnitz, who were unfortunately relegated to the regional league. The next season, although Chemnitz missed out on promotion, Ballack played in every game and scored 10 goals. His talent was spotted by 1. FC Kaiserslautern coach Otto Rehhagel and Ballack was signed by the newly promoted club in time for the start of the 1997/98 season.

He made his full first team debut on 28 March 1998 and eventually played in 16 games for Kaiserslautern that season, as they became the first ever newly promoted team to win the Bundesliga.

The next season he made 30 appearances, including games in the Champions League.

On 1 July 1999, Bayer Leverkusen signed Ballack for 4.4 million euros. He was 22 years old.

This is where he really made his name and broke onto the world stage.

Given an attacking midfield role by coaches Daum and Toppmöller, he was a member of the Leverkusen side which came agonisingly close to winning the Bundesliga in 2000 - indeed an own goal from Ballack helped send the team to a 2:0 defeat to Unterhaching on the last day of the season.

He was also a member of the Leverkusen team in 2002 - the infamous year when the club narrowly missed winning the Bundesliga, and lost the DFB Cup and UEFA Champions League finals, despite having played wonderful football all season.

Real Madrid and Bayern Munich were both very interested in signing Ballack and in 2002 he signed for the Bavarians for a fee of 12.9 million euros. In his four seasons there the club won three Bundesliga and DFB Cup doubles. Ballack scored 44 goals and made 107 appearances.

Ballack's next move was to the English Premiership when he joined Chelsea on a free transfer. He arrived in London in 2006 and stayed until 2010. Ballack made 166 appearances, scored 25 goals and won the Premiership, the League Cup and the FA Cup. He was a member of the Chelsea squad that were runners up in the 2008 Champions League final.

In 2010 Ballack returned to Bayer Leverkusen for what were to be the last two years of his career. Within months of signing, he sustained a shin injury which would keep him from playing for the rest of the year. Although he was back in action by February 2011, he retired in 2012.

Ballack first appeared for the national team in April 1999 and only played for 63 minutes in the ill-fated Euro 2000 campaign.

He was a key member of the German team which reached the final of the 2002 World Cup. Ballack was included in the FIFA World Cup All-Star Team.

He was German captain for Euro 2004.

Ballack was a member of the 2006 World Cup team and was included for the second time in the FIFA World Cup All-Star Team.

He captained Germany in the 2008 Euro Championship and was included in the Team of the Tournament.

He played his last games for Germany in the 2010 World Cup qualifiers, but then missed the finals through injury.

With 42 goals, Ballack is Germany's 8th highest goal scorer ever. He made 98 appearances for the national team.

Since retiring as a player, Michael Ballack has worked as a TV pundit for the BBC, Sky and ESPN.

Honours

Club

Bayer Leverkusen

Bundesliga Runner-up: 2002, 2011

DFB-Pokal Runner-up: 2002

UEFA Champions League Runner-up: 2002

Bayern Munich

Bundesliga: 2003, 2005, 2006

DFB Cup: 2003, 2005, 2006

DFB League Cup: 2004

Chelsea

League Cup: 2007

League Cup Runner-up: 2008

FA Cup: 2007, 2009, 2010

UEFA Champions League Runner-up: 2008

FA Community Shield: 2009

FA Community Shield Runner-up: 2006

Premier League: 2010

International

FIFA World Cup Runner-up: 2002

FIFA World Cup Third Place: 2006

UEFA European Championship Runner-up: 2008

FIFA Confederations Cup Third Place: 2005

Individual honours

UEFA Club Midfielder of the Year: 2002

UEFA Team of the Year: 2002

ESM Team of the Year: 2002

German Footballer of the Year: 2002, 2003, 2005

Kicker Player of the Year: 2002

Most assists in the 2002 FIFA World Cup

FIFA World Cup All-star team: 2002, 2006

FIFA XI: 2002

UEFA Euro Team of the Tournament: 2004, 2008

Bayer Leverkusen Squad of the Century

FIFA Confederations Cup Silver Boot Winner: 2005

2008 Goal of the Year in Germany

∿

René Adler

René Adler is one of the most talented goalkeepers in a country famous for its goalkeepers. He was born in Leipzig and played for Hamburger SV and Mainz. But it was at Bayer 04 Leverkusen that he shot to prominence.

He began playing football at the age of 6, working his way through the youth teams of VfB Leipzig. Spotted by scouts from Bayer Leverkusen, he joined the club's youth system in 2000.

One problem he faced when he came to Leverkusen was where to live. Leipzig was a long way from home, and he was too young to live on his own. Longstanding goalkeeper and newly appointed goalkeeping coach Rüdiger Vollborn took him in with his own family, where he was to stay for the next four years.

Although included in the first team squad in 2003/04, he did not make his Bundesliga debut until February 2007, when he was drafted in to replace Hans-Jörg But, who had been suspended following a red card. This first game was against league leaders Schalke 04, who had not been beaten for 13 games. Adler saved at least ten shots and his 'world class saves' were singled out for praise from manager Michael Skibbe. Leverkusen won the game 1:0 thanks to a breakaway goal by Stefan Kießling, but even in the dying seconds of the game Adler had to produce a double-save to make sure Leverkusen hung on.

Kicker magazine raved about this debut performance and nominated him 'Man of the day'. Adler had arrived and went on to have a superb season,

Once established in the team, Adler was to be the first choice keeper at Leverkusen for the next four years. He was Bundesliga Goalkeeper of the Year 2008 and a key member of the squads that reached the 2009 DFB Cup Final and finished second in the Bundesliga season 2010/11.

Injury then kept him out of the game for a long period and he lost his position as the club's top keeper to recruit Bernd Leno. Although Leverkusen were keen to renew his contract, Adler eventually left the club in 2012, moving to Hamburger SV on a free transfer. He had been at Leverkusen for 12 years.

He made 117 appearances at Hamburg. His last save of 2015 actually kept Hamburg in the Bundesliga. Hamburg had ended the season third from bottom and therefore had to play two games against Karlsruhe, who had finished third in the 2 Bundesliga. In the second game, with seconds of added time remaining, Hamburg were hanging onto a 2:1 lead - enough to give them victory over the two games. Then Karlsruhe were awarded a penalty. Adler saved the spot kick and with it Hamburg's top tier status.

Adler spent the last two years of his playing career with Mainz.

Adler played for the German Under-19 and Under-21 teams and was part of the national squad that reached the finals of Euro 2008. He made his first team debut for Germany in October 2008 in a world cup qualifying match. After the retirement of Jens Lehmann and the death of Robert Enke, he became Germany's first choice keeper throughout the qualifying games for the 2010 World Cup and played 11 games for the national side. He was confirmed as the number one for the finals. Unfortunately, because of a rib injury, he did not go to South Africa and only played for Germany once more.

Despite some excellent performances with Hamburger SV he was not selected to go to the World Cup finals in 2014 in Brazil.

Journalist Ronald Reng has written a moving book about goalkeeper Robert Enke, who tragically took his own life in 2009. It's called 'A Life Too Short: The tragedy of Robert Enke', and it contains several passages about Adler, who, alongside Enke and Neuer, was one of the top three German goalkeepers of the time.

~

Rudi Völler

It is fitting that the chapter on Leverkusen heroes ends with Rudi Völler, one of Germany's best ever footballers, a former Leverkusen player, and Director of Sport since 2005.

Völler, who was born in 1960, is one of only three people who has appeared in a World Cup final as both a player (1986 and 1990) and a manager (2002). Over a 12 year period, he appeared 90 times for the German national team and scored 47 goals. He played at the top level in Germany, Italy and France, scoring 257 goals. For most of the 1980s, he was considered to be Germany's top striker. He rarely scored spectacular goals, but he was excellent with the ball at his feet and could take on defenders.

Völler played football for the youth teams of his local home club TSV Hanau from the age of 8. He moved to the youth team of Kickers Offenbach in 1975. Offenbach wanted to give him a full-time contract as soon as he left school - but his mother insisted he completed an apprenticeship first. He continued to train at Offenbach and first played for the senior team in 1977. The next season, he signed his first professional contract and stayed with Offenbach until 1980.

After a spell with 1860 München, Völler then signed for Bundesliga club Werder Bremen in 1982. The 1982/83 season was a very successful one for Völler. He was the top scorer in the Bundesliga and was named German Footballer of the Year. He won his first cap for the German national team.

In 1987 he transferred to A.S. Roma. Nicknamed 'il tedesco volante' (the flying German) by the fans, he became the mainstay of the team. He was the club's top scorer in several seasons and in 1991 won the Italian cup.

A move to Olympique Marseille followed in 1992. He was signed to replace their superstar striker, Jean-Pierre Papin. He scored 24 goals for Marseille and won the Champions League with them in 1993. Unfortunately, Marseille's involvement in a bribery scandal led to the club being stripped of its 1993 league title and relegated to the second division in 1994.

Völler returned to Germany in 1994 when he signed for Bayer 04 Leverkusen, where he spent the last two years of his playing career.

Rudi Völler also had a highly successful international career. Amongst the 47 goals he scored for the national team were 8 in World Cup final rounds.

He played in three UEFA European Championships and three World Cup finals and was a member of the German team which won the World Cup in 1990.

When Völler finally ended his playing career, he stayed with Bayer Leverkusen, working as their Director of Sport until 2000.

Following Germany's woeful performance in the 2000 UEFA Cup finals, Völler was drafted in to replace Erich Ribbeck as coach to the national team. Although his Germany team achieved second place in the 2002 World Cup finals. He resigned in 2004 after the team was eliminated in the group stage from the World Cup finals.

In 2004 he had a very brief spell as manager with AS Roma and in 2005 returned to Bayer Leverkusen as Director of Sport, a post he still holds He has twice acted as interim manager for short periods at Leverkusen.

Honours

Club

Roma

Coppa Italia: 1991

UEFA Cup Runner-up: 1991

Marseille

UEFA Champions League: 1993

International

FIFA World Cup: 1990

FIFA World Cup Runner-up: 1986

UEFA European Championship Runner-up: 1992

Individual honours

UEFA European Under-21 Football Championship Golden Player: 1982

2. Bundesliga Top Goalscorer: 1981–82

Bundesliga Top Goalscorer: 1982–83

German Footballer of the Year: 1983

UEFA Euro Team of the Tournament: 1984

UEFA Cup Top Goalscorer: 1990–91

A.S. Roma Hall of Fame: 2014

Manager

FIFA World Cup Runner-up: 2002

6

PRACTICAL INFORMATION

Getting there, buying tickets and finding somewhere to stay

If you've never been to a German football match before, or if you are looking for a light introduction to the modern Bundesliga, I think a trip to Bayer 04 Leverkusen is one of the best places to start.

Buying tickets

The simplest way to get tickets is to call the club's ticket hotline (0049 1805 040404). There is always someone there who can speak English and who can advise you on the best places to sit. You could also use the Online Shop. Although this is in German, it is easy to work out what you need to do. This way you can choose exactly where to sit and you can use the Print@Home facility to print your ticket before you leave.

An easy city to reach

Leverkusen is between Düsseldorf and Cologne and you can get there easily and quickly by train from either city. For example, the journey from Düsseldorf with the regional train (RE1 or RE5) takes about 15 minutes and there are at least three trains an hour.

A pleasant city to visit

Leverkusen is an attractive and very modern city with plenty of green spaces and lots of cafes, bars and shops. There is plenty to do and see before or after a game, or indeed to entertain non-fans while you are watching the football.

A fantastic stadium built for football fans

The approach to the BayArena is one of the most straight-forward and pleasant routes to a ground in Europe - and you can get there on foot. From the station you follow the signs for Sportpark and BayArena through a wooded park. After about 15 minutes, the stadium appears through the trees on your right.

It looks good, but it's also a great place to watch football. Extensive modernisation has turned it into one of the most attractive, comfortable and fan-friendly venues you are ever likely to visit.

With a maximum capacity of 30,000, there are enough fans to generate a sense of occasion without it being over-whelming.

And the closeness of all seats to the action makes sure everyone gets a good view and maximises the atmosphere.

Inside the stadium there are plenty of food and drink outlets, a club shop, a creche and free Wi-Fi. If you download the Live-App you can even access live, real-time data about the game. All the facilities are well maintained.

Visitors welcome

The club has an open and welcoming ethos. Signs are in English and German and teams of helpers are on hand to offer advice. The club has decorated the barriers dividing home and away fans to recognise the contribution visitors make to a good game.

You can't use cash

You can pay for food and drink with your credit card, Apple Pay or Google Pay. But they don't accept cash payments.

Where to stay and what else to do

Leverkusen is easy to get to from both Cologne and Düsseldorf, so you could base yourself in one of these fine cities and do a spot of sightseeing, shopping or dining out before and after the football.

Leverkusen itself has a nice shopping mall in the city centre and there are plenty of pubs.

The Lindner is a 200-room hotel connected to the BayArena. There are, however, cheaper alternatives.

- Hotel ibis
- Hotel am Stadion
- Haus Fück

You can, of course, get more information at the Leverkusen Tourist Information website.

7

FINDING OUT MORE ABOUT GERMAN FOOTBALL

Watching German football live is excellent value for money. Even so, travel and hotel costs mount up, and so those of us not lucky enough to live in Germany often have to follow the football from afar. So here are a few places you might go to for extra information.

~

Websites

The **Bundesliga** has a website in English where you can get the latest stories as well as information on fixtures and scores. It has detailed and very informative sections for each club. You can sign up for a newsletter, and there is also a dedicated **Bundesliga channel** on YouTube and a **Bundesliga App**.

- https://www.bundesliga.com/en/
- https://www.youtube.com/user/bundesliga

- https://www.bundesliga.com/en/fanzone/app/

Deutsche Welle is an international broadcaster. The English language website provides German and international news, as well as background videos and articles, links to TV programmes and German language courses. The Sports section includes reports and discussion on German football.

- http://www.dw.com/en/top-stories/s-9097

Sky shows top Bundesliga fixtures each week. **BT Sport** has exclusive rights to the Champions League and Europa League, which feature plenty of German teams.

Vavel is an international online sports paper. The German section has articles, match reports and transfer news.

- https://www.vavel.com/en/international-football/

Bleacher report is another online sports paper with plenty of current Bundesliga news and stories.

- http://bleacherreport.com/germany

The Bundesliga section of broadcaster **ESPN**'s website provides news, match reports, video clips and discussions.

- http://www.espn.co.uk/

Kicker is a very popular sports magazine. Although everything on its website is in German, you can pick up loads of information about fixtures, results and standings. It's ideal for planning a trip.

- https://www.kicker.de/

≈

Blogs, podcasts and a fanzine

Outside Write - podcasts and articles about travel and football abroad, including plenty on Germany.

- http://outsidewrite.co.uk/category/germany/

Talking Fussball - a weekly podcast from Munich.

- http://talkingfussball.com/

Halb Vier is an English fanzine dedicated to all aspects of German football, including stadiums, fans, club histories and much more. You can order it here.

- https://halbvier.bigcartel.com/

Football Weekends is a magazine covering football tourism across the UK and Europe.

- https://footballweekends.co.uk/

≈

Apps and Social Media

Futbology is the perfect app for any football trip, and I can't recommend it strongly enough. It contains a database of more than 25,000 stadiums and has up-to-date fixture lists for more than 700 leagues. In the Germany section, you can find information about clubs and games right down to the 6th tier. My favourite feature is the Matches Nearby tool, which tells you which games are on near where you happen to be. You can get this brilliant app for iOS and Android.

- https://apps.apple.com/gb/app/groundhopper/id489247406
- https://play.google.com/store/apps/details?id=com.kepermat.groundhopper&hl=en_UK

European Football Weekends is a Facebook group whose members share information and stories about watching football across Europe and beyond. No matter which club you want to watch, you will find someone here with detailed local knowledge.

- https://www.facebook.com/groups/europeanfootballweekends/

Bundesliga clubs have Facebook groups and Twitter feeds in English.

Books

It's a case of quality rather than quantity when it comes to books about German football. There aren't that many, but the ones that are available are excellent.

If you read no other book about football in Germany, you should read **Tor! The Story of German Football**, by Uli Hesse. This well-researched book takes the reader through the history of German football, from its origins in the late 19th century to the present day.

There's a whole chapter on how German clubs got their names, and the story of football unfolds within the context of German history. Hesse describes how in the early days clubs had to fight for respectability in the face of opposition from the gymnastics movement, but how football gathered momentum and became a mass sport in the 1920s and 1930s. He outlines the horrors of the Nazi regime and war years and their impact on football and then goes on to the 'Miracle of Bern' when Germany won the World Cup. He covers the building of dominant sides in the '60s and 70's, the TV explosion of the late '80s, and then the low point of Euro 2000. The book ends with a description of the inexorable rise of German football from 2000 to become the world force it is today.

It is written in a very accessible style, and Hesse makes brilliant use of stories to bring facts to life.

Hesse has published two more books about German football. **Building the Yellow Wall** tells the story of Borussia Dortmund.

Bayern: Creating a Global Superclub narrates the rise and rise of Bayern Munich.

Raphael Honigstein speaks and writes knowledgeably, fluently and interestingly about football in German and English.

In **Das Reboot: How German Football Reinvented Itself and Conquered the World**, he charts German football's return from the wilderness of the late 1990s, culminating in the glorious victories over Brazil and Argentina in the 2014 World Cup finals.

Matchdays: The Hidden Story of the Bundesliga by Ronald Reng tells the story of the Bundesliga through the life and times of Heinz Höher. His career as a player spanned the years before and after the formation of the Bundesliga. He played for Bayer 04 Leverkusen, Meidericher SV (later renamed MSV Duisburg), FC Twente and VfL Bochum. As a coach he worked for VfL Bochum, Schwarz Weiß Essen, MSV Duisburg, Fortuna Düsseldorf and FC Nürnberg, as well as teams in Greece and Saudi Arabia.

The reader experiences the history of the Bundesliga from the perspective of someone who lived it. This approach also enables Reng to give great insights into everyday life in modern Germany.

Höher himself is a fascinating and at times tragic figure. The many bitter disappointments in his life story leave the reader in no doubt about the cruelty of modern football and the narrow line between success and failure.

Robert Reng was a close friend of Robert Enke, the German goalkeeper who tragically took his own life in 2009. In **A**

Life Too Short: The Tragedy of Robert Enke, Reng describes his friend's life, casting light on the crushing pressures of professional sport.

The Miracle Of Bern is a film, not a book – but it's the best film I have ever come across about German football. Set in the gloomy post-war years when Germany was still coming to terms with its terrible past and only just recovering from the disasters inflicted on the country by National Socialism, it leads up to Germany's surprising victory in the 1954 World Cup. The film is much more than an intensely emotional and touching story. It shows us what Germany was like in the immediate post-war years and what football was like before the Bundesliga.

If you want to get into the culture and tradition of one team, **Pirates, Punks & Politics: FC St. Pauli: Falling in Love with a Radical Football Club** by Nick Davidson is the book for you. Davidson describes his development from a disillusioned ex-Watford fan, through troubled times following non-league football, to his discovery of and love affair with St Pauli. He explains how he moved from interested outsider to a regular part of the fan scene. The context for this personal journey is provided by a description of the transformation of St Pauli into a unique football club, which in turn is set within the recent history of Hamburg and Germany.

The result is a fascinating insight into the culture and traditions of a cult club, and an intriguing glimpse of how football could be if the clubs were genuinely run for and by the fans, and fully embedded in the communities they serve.

Trautman's Journey: From Hitler Youth to FA Cup Legend is the biography of the famous Manchester City goalkeeper

Bert Trautmann. Although Trautmann achieved fame and fortune in English football, the book provides a fascinating picture of life in Hitler's Germany and of how the Nazi regime managed to indoctrinate young people.

The Ball is Round: A Global History of Football by David Goldblatt tells the story of football across the world. It shows the origins, development and social significance of German football in a European and global context.

The People's Game by Alan McDougal made it to the Guardian's list of best sports books of 2016. McDougal is History and European studies professor at the University of Guelph. In this book, he explains how attempts by the communist dictatorship to use football for political ends failed.

8

REFERENCES

Books

Bayer 04 Leverkusen Die Fussball-Chronik
Alex Feuerherdt (ISBN 978-3-89544-819-9)
111 Gründe, Bayer 04 Leverkusen zu lieben: Eine Liebeserklärung an den großartigsten Fußballverein der Welt
Jens Peters (ISBN 978-3862652679)
Die Mannchschaft aus dem Haberland Stadion TSV Bayer Leverkusen
Jens Novotny Carsten Ramjelow Bernd Schneider (ISBN 978-3-7386-8503-9)
Tor! The Story of German Football
Uli Hesse (ISBN 978-0-9561011-3-6)
Das Reboot : How German Football reinvented itself
Raphael Honigstein (Epub ISBN 9781473521803)
A Life Too Short : The tragedy of Robert Enke
Ronald Reng (Epub ISBN 9781446499023)
Matchdays: The Hidden Story of the Bundesliga
Ronald Reng (ISBN 978-1-47113-649-8)

Germany 1945
Richard Bessel (ISBN 978-1-41652-619-3)

Websites and blogs

Neverkusen Podcast
https://www.neverkusen-podcast.net/
Bayer 04 Leverkusen official website
https://www.bayer04.de/en-us/
Bayer 04 Leverkusen Facebook Page
https://www.facebook.com/bayer04leverkusen/
The Leverkusen section of the Bundesliga website
https://www.bundesliga.com/en/bundesliga/clubs/bayer-04-leverkusen/news

Articles

Der sympathische Plastikklub: Die Zeit Online
https://www.zeit.de/sport/2013-02/bayer-leverkusen-dortmund-vollborn?utm_referrer=https%3A%2F%2Fwww.google.com%2F
Bayer Leverkusen - Stepping out of the shadows: Sports Interactive Community
https://community.sigames.com/forums/topic/295968-fm14-bayer-leverkusen-stepping-out-of-the-shadows/
History of Bayer
https://www.bayer.com/en/history
Bernd Schuster: The impossible German maverick : These Football Times
https://thesefootballtimes.co/2015/03/20/bernd-schuster-a-real-german-maverick/
Michael Ballack - Nearly man or midfield genius?:

Guardian
https://www.theguardian.com/football/blog/2013/jun/05/
michael-ballack-nearly-man-genius

YouTube

Zidane's goal in the 2002 Champions League Final
https://www.youtube.com/watch?v=4TuggkDPw6A
Kießling's ghost goal
https://www.youtube.com/watch?v=vQZmRqxnH6M
René Adler's top five saves
https://www.youtube.com/watch?v=dweYHuH70C0

9

FINAL WORDS

I hope you have found this guide interesting and helpful and that you enjoyed reading it as much as I enjoyed writing it.

I would love to hear from you if you have ideas for future projects or if you have come across a great website or book about German football.

For more information
www.bundesligaandbeyond.net
johnalder@bundesligaandbeyond.net

ALSO BY JOHN ALDER

Discovering German Football

Are you planning a football trip to Germany? This short guide will help you plan your trip and decide which clubs to visit. There is also key information on every club in the top three divisions as well as links to the best books, websites, blogs and podcasts.

The Football Tourist's Guide to the German Ruhrgebiet

Bordered by the rivers Rhine, Ruhr and Lippe the Ruhrgebiet is one of Germany's 'hidden gems'. A vibrant, exciting and thoroughly modern metropolis, it is steeped in history and tradition. nFor over 100 years it has also been the beating heart of German football.

This guidebook introduces its major cities and towns, the history, culture and traditions of its people and its football clubs. There is advice on how to plan a visit and where to find out more.

Borussia Mönchengladbach: an introduction

This book sets out to share the history, tradition, triumphs and disappointments of this great club with the English-speaking world. The book tells the story of Borussia from its foundation in 1900 to the present day. As well as biographies of former players and managers and famous anecdotes, there is a wealth of background information for English speakers considering a visit to Germany or wanting to follow the club from afar.

FC Schalke 04: an introduction

In 1904 a group of young miners from Gelsenkirchen got together to play football. They had very little money, no kit to wear, no ball to play with. They didn't even have a pitch to play on. This book tells the story of how the club these young men formed grew to become **FC Schalke 04**, one of the biggest, wealthiest and best-known football clubs in the world.

Printed in Great Britain
by Amazon

34644937R00048